STRAIGHT FROM THE STREETS

AS REAL AS IT GETS AFFIRMATIONS

Arlene McKenzie

ISBN: 9798639534126 (paperback)

Printed in the United States of America

RELATIVES ARE PEOPLE LIKE EVERYONE ELSE

THEY TOO MAKE MISTAKES

EVERY SECOND COUNTS

ONCE IT PASSES, IT NEVER RETURNS

ALWAYS BE OPEN TO HEAR WHAT YOUR CHILD HAS TO SAY

IF YOU WON'T LISTEN SOMEONE ELSE WILL

DON'T LET YOUR EGO GET THE BEST OF YOU

WHERE CROWD GATHERS

TROUBLE LINGERS

BEFORE YOU HURT SOMEONE

REMEMBER YOUR LOVED ONES

BECAUSE WHAT FALLS OFF THE HEAD

FALLS ON THE SHOULDER

OPPOSITIONS WILL COME

AND I WILL STAND FIRM

SOMETIMES OUR BIGGEST HATERS

ARE THE ONES WE LAY WITH

IF YOU MUST FIGHT

KEEP YOUR EYES ON YOUR OPPOSITION

TIME TAKES CARE OF EVERYTHING

ALWAYS BE AWARE OF YOUR ENVIRONMENT

BE CAREFUL OF ANYONE WHO ALWAYS AGREES

WITH EVERYTHING YOU SAY OR DO

IF YOU FEEL IT'S IMPOSSIBLE

DO IT ANYWAY

EXPECT THE BEST

PREPARE FOR THE WORST

WHEN INVITED ANYWHERE, EVEN IF YOU WERE SPONSORED

ALWAYS HAVE CASH FOR CAB

IN CASE SOMETHING GOES WRONG

IT TOOK TEN YEARS TO BUILD THAT MANSION

YET ONLY TEN MINUTES FOR IT TO BURN TO ASHES

WORRYING WILL NEVER HELP WORRYING

INSTEAD OF SHOUTING AT SOMEONE

WHO CARES ZERO FOR WHAT YOU ARE SAYING

WHY NOT TALK TO THE TREES OF NATURE

THEY'LL NEVER TURN YOU DOWN

YOUR BEST REVENGE IS YOUR SUCCESS

IT'S TIME TO BURY THAT ILLUSIVE VERSION OF YOU

AND ALLOW THE NEW AND TRANSFORMED YOU TO BE BORN

NEVER LET YOUR PAST OVERSHADOW YOUR FUTURE

STRUGGLES EITHER BUILD YOU

OR BREAK YOU

NOT SHARING THE SAME INTEREST

DOESN'T MAKE THE OTHER PERSON IRRELEVANT

WEARING CLEAN CLOTHES

DOES NOT MEAN THE HEART'S CLEAN

THERE ARE MANY WAYS TO CATCH A FISH

KNOW WHO BRINGS YOU TO OPEN BODIES OF WATER

ESPECIALLY IF YOU CANNOT SWIM

YOU MIGHT NOT BE THE PRETTIEST

BUT ALWAYS REMEMBER

THAT THERE'S SOMEONE OUT THERE

LESS PRETTIER THAN YOU

WHAT MORE THAN ONE PERSON KNOWS

IS NO LONGER A SECRET

THE BIBLE TEACHES US TO LOVE MEN

NOT TO TRUST THEM

LET YOUR LIGHT SHINE

RESPECT YOUR ELDERS

STAND UP FOR YOUR CHILDREN

CORRECT THEM BEHIND CLOSED DOORS

LIFE'S TOUGH

BUT

YOU GOT TO KEEP ON PUSHING

IF YOU WANT THE CHANGE

BE THE CHANGE

YOU CONQUER THE BATTLE OF THE SPIRIT

YOU CONQUER ALL

TRANSITION CAN BE SCARY

YOU MIGHT FEEL LIKE YOU NO LONGER BELONG THERE

THAT'S BECAUSE YOU DON'T

IN TIMES OF CRISIS

YOU WILL KNOW WHO REALLY HAS YOUR BACK

THERE IS A WARRIOR

DEEP DOWN INSIDE OF YOU

INTUITION IS QUITE POWERFUL

THE SAME ONE WHOM RISES THE SUN

IS THE SAME ONE WHOM BRINGS IT DOWN

A WORD OF ENCOURAGEMENT

CAN BE A BLESSING

SOME YOU'LL DISH SUGAR

YET THEY'LL DISH YOU SALT

NOTHING CUTS DEEPER THAN TO IGNORE SOMEONE

WHO'S EXPECTING A REACTION

CERTAIN THINGS ARE

SIMPLY OUT OF YOUR CONTROL

LET'S PUT A PICTURE TO THAT THOUGHT

AND MAKE IT A REALITY

WHERE DOES YOUR PRIORITIES LIE?

SOME PEOPLE AREN'T

ALWAYS WHAT THEY SEEM

THE WORLD DOES NOT REVOLVE AROUND

WHAT THEY MIGHT THINK

YOUR SANITY IS

WHAT MATTERS

ASSOCIATE YOURSELF WITH PEOPLE WHO HEAR YOUR CRY

EVEN WHEN YOU'VE NOT YET SPOKEN

WHEN THE HIGH IS DOWN AND THE FUN IS OVER

THE REAL PROBLEM STILL STANDS

BE STRONG IN YOUR DAY OF FAMINE BECAUSE

WHEN YOUR DAY OF REAPING COMES

YOUR FRUITS SHALL BE MANY

THERE'S NOTHING CASUAL

ABOUT A PRAYER FOR PURPOSE

TODAY IS ANOTHER OPPORTUNITY

TO RIGHT THE WRONGS OF YESTERDAY

TRANSITION COMES WITH CHALLENGES

BE READY

NOT EVERYONE DESERVES

YOUR EMOTIONS

LET'S START CONVERTING

NEGATIVES TO POSITIVES

RELATIONSHIP EQUALS

COMPROMISE

CAN'T BE ONE-SIDED

WHEN THEY SAY YOU CAN'T

MAKE THAT YOUR MOTIVATION

DON'T BE TOO PREDICTABLE

MAKE THEM WONDER WHAT YOU'RE THINKING

FREE YOURSELF FROM ALL THINGS

HOLDING YOU CAPTIVE

THE WONDERFUL LIFE THE DEVIL HAS DESIGNED FOR YOU

IS JUST AN ILLUSION

THERE ARE BILLIONS OF PEOPLE IN THIS WORLD

SOMEONE WILL NOT LIKE YOU

MISERY

LOVES

COMPANY

I COULD HAVE, I SHOULD HAVE, WAS THEN

I CAN AND I WILL, IS NOW

JUST FOR THE SAKE OF BREATHING

IS A REASON TO GIVE THANKS

TEACH THE CHILDREN THE DIFFERENCE BETWEEN

WHAT'S TRENDING FROM WHAT'S RIGHT

I BELIEVE IN YOU

DO YOU BELIEVE IN YOU?

IF YOU DIDN'T PREPARE FOR YOUR CHILD'S FUTURE

MAKE IT A PRIORITY

TO PREPARE THAT CHILD FOR THE FUTURE

START MAKING A

PLAN TODAY

SEPARATE YOURSELF

FROM ALL MIGRAINES

IF THE SPACE IS NOT SAFE

TAKE IT TO THE LORD

DON'T CURSE

WHERE YOU ARE COMING FROM

FOCUS ON WHERE YOU ARE GOING

SNAKES ALSO COMES

IN FORM OF PEOPLE

START VIEWING YOUR SITUATION

AS A CHALLENGE AND NOT A PROBLEM

BEING DRAGGED THROUGH THE DIRT AND GUTTER

NEVER DEFINES WHO YOU ARE

NEVER FORGET THE ONES WHO GAVE YOU HOPE

IN YOUR HARD TIMES

EVERYONE HAS THEIR STORY

SO YOURS COULD HAVE NEVER BEEN MINE

MEN WHO HURT WOMEN

ARE WEAK EXAMPLES OF MEN

THERE'S MUCH YOU CAN LEARN

BY STUDYING BODY LANGUAGE

SOMETIMES YOUR CIRCLE NEEDS TO BE A MIXED VARIETY

YOU NEVER KNOW WHERE YOU MIGHT HAVE A FLAT TIRE

IT DOES NOT MATTER WHAT YOUR EARS HEAR

LISTEN TO WHAT THEIR EYES ARE SAYING

CELEBRATE YOUR RECOVERY

EVERY LITTLE COUNTS

A HOUSE CANNOT BE BUILT

WITHOUT STARTING A FOUNDATION

WHEN THEY GOSSIP ABOUT YOU

HOLD YOUR HEAD HIGH

IT MEANS YOU'RE IMPORTANT

SWALLOW YOUR PRIDE AND TAKE WHAT YOU GET

UNTIL YOU GET WHAT YOU WANT

TO WHOM MUCH IS GIVEN

MUCH IS REQUIRED

WHEN I REWIND TO WHERE I'M COMING FROM

AND FAST FORWARD TO WHERE I AM TODAY

I AM INDEED BLESSED

LET'S BREAK THE SILENCE OF DEPRESSION

RIGHT NOW

TAKE SOME TIME OFF JUST FOR YOU

APPRECIATE YOURSELF

THERE'S ONLY ONE YOU

TEACH YOUR CHILD ABOUT STD'S AND SAFE SEX

BETTER SAFE THAN SORRY

BE WITH SOMEONE WHO HAS A FLAW

THAT YOU CAN LIVE WITH

SOME PROBLEMS YOU WALK AWAY FROM

SOME YOU RUN AWAY FROM

SOME YOU TRY REASONING OUT

SOME YOU WORK YOUR WAY AROUND

CHOOSE YOUR BATTLES WISELY

FORGIVENESS IS NOT BEING WEAK

IT'S TAKING BACK YOUR POWER

FROM WHOEVER DONE YOU WRONG

DON'T LET YOUR TONGUE LEAD YOU

TO YOUR DEATH

KEEP DOMESTIC AFFAIRS

OUT OF CHILDREN'S SIGHT

IF YOU'RE HAVING A HANGOVER

SUCK ON A LIME

NEVER WASTE FIVE YEARS OF YOUR LIFE

IN A RELATIONSHIP WITH SOMEONE

YOU DON'T SEE A FUTURE WITH

GIVE TO OTHERS WHO NEED IT MORE

THAN YOU DO

NEVER ANSWER TO THE FIRST CALL

YOU NEVER KNOW

JUST WHO MIGHT BE OUT THERE

THERE'S A TIME AND PLACE FOR EVERYTHING

WEARING THE SAME STRONG FRAGRANCE CONSISTENTLY

IS NOT WISE

BECAUSE SOMEONE COULD EASILY TRACK YOU

CHOOSE YOUR BATTLES WISELY

YOU HAVE THE POWER

TO BE ANYTHING YOU WANT TO BE

IF YOUR ROOMMATE IS NOT ACTING RIGHT

MOVE WITHOUT GIVING NOTICE

SAVE YOURSELF FROM HARM

WHEN THE DOG WIGGLES ITS TAIL, IT'S A FRIEND

WHEN THE DOG'S TAIL STANDS STIFF, IT'S DANGER

IT'S OKAY TO SAY

NO

START LOOKING AT THINGS

FROM A DIFFERENT ANGLE

IF YOU MUST DRINK ALCOHOL

KNOW YOUR LIMITS

THE ONLY TIME I LOOK BACK

IS TO SEE HOW FAR I'VE COME

LET GO

AND

LET GOD

DON'T LET YOUR MIND

LEAD YOU ASTRAY

MAY GOD OPEN

MY SPIRITUAL EYES

I PROCLAIM VICTORY

AND

PROSPERITY OVER MY LIFE

CAREFUL WHAT YOU

WISH

FOR

DRUGS IS THE DEVIL'S GAME

WIN IT WITH GOD

IF YOU CAN'T SAY GOOD

SAY NOTHING

IF YOU DON'T FEEL WELCOME

YOU SHOULD LEAVE

PEOPLE WILL TREAT YOU

HOW YOU ALLOW THEM TO

BE MINDFUL OF THE CONVERSATIONS

YOU ENTERTAIN

IF SOMEONE KEEPS REMINDING YOU

OF YOUR TERRIBLE PAST

RUN!

BE NICE

BECAUSE LIFE IS FULL OF SURPRISES

STRAIGHTEN UP YOUR MESS

BEFORE YOU TALK ABOUT SOMEONE'S MESS

SOMETIMES WE MUST CHOOSE TO HAVE

SELECTIVE HEARING

NOT EVERYONE IS ALLOWED

TO SPEAK INTO YOUR LIFE

RUB YOUR MAN'S FEET

MAKE HIM FEEL LIKE A KING

BRING YOUR LADY FLOWERS OR RUB HER BACK

MAKE HER FEEL LIKE A QUEEN

TEACH YOUR CHILDREN TO PRAY

SO THEY CAN PUT FIRE ON THE DEVIL THEMSELVES

KNOW THE STREET CODES

BECAUSE THIS WORLD IS FULL OF TRICKY

LUST IS NOT

LOVE

WINNING MEANS

MAKING SACRIFICES

PEOPLE WILL REMIND YOU OF WHAT YOU COULDN'T DO

TO DISCREDIT YOUR TRUE POTENTIAL

ABOUT THE AUTHOR

Arlene McKenzie is a sweet, humble individual, with a receptive spirit. She is the definition of a strong black woman. Her journey has been quite a tough one, but she kept on fighting and lives to celebrate her victory by the grace of God.